Internet Marketing

Secrets of Online Sales Success!

by

Owen Jones

Copyright

Published by
Megan Publishing Services
https://meganthemisconception.com

Hello and thank you for buying this book called 'Internet Marketing: Secrets of Online Marketing Success!'.

Welcome to this introduction to Internet Marketing your guide to unlocking the dynamic world of online promotion and business growth. As an authority in Internet marketing, I am delighted to accompany you on this journey to harness the immense potential of digital strategies.

In an era where the Internet is at the heart of commerce and communication, understanding the intricacies of Internet marketing is essential for success. This manual has been crafted with precision to equip beginners with the fundamental knowledge needed to navigate this ever-evolving landscape. Each piece of advice and strategy is grounded in accuracy and the latest industry standards.

From unravelling the core concepts of SEO, social media, and content marketing, to demystifying the art of online advertising and analytics, we will cover it comprehensively. Embracing Internet marketing doesn't just mean leveraging technology – it's about delivering value, building relationships, and fostering trust. By embarking on this educational voyage, you are poised to make impactful strides in the digital realm while upholding the principles of honesty and authenticity. Let's dive into the realm of Internet marketing and pave the way for your digital success.

I hope that you will find the contents helpful, useful and profitable.

The information in this ebook on various aspects of using the Internet to your advantage is organised into 20 chapters of about 500-600 words each.

I hope that it will interest those who are hoping to make money on line. In fact, the number of people trying to make (some extra) money online has skyrocketed over the last ten or twelve years, but especially since the Covid-19 lockdowns.

Not everything can be blamed on Covid-19 though. Britain, for example, has suffered twelve years of 'austerity' brought in by a government that seems no longer to care about the electorate. First they blamed the banking crisis; then the influx of foreign labour; then Covid; and now Brexit and the war in the Ukraine. No doubt you have heard similar excuses where you live. Anyway, the result has been exorbitant inflation and a reduction in wages, and that has led to enterprising people trying improve their situation by working online. This book is for you. I hope that it helps.

If you have any feedback, please leave it with the company you bought this book from.

Thanks again for purchasing this book,

Regards,

Owen Jones

Table of Contents

1. Article Marketing Tips

Many individuals who create their first web site get a rude surprise after launching it. They spend a long time thinking about making a website, a long time learning how to create one and a long time making it. They launch it and wait for visitors to flock to it. And nothing happens. No-one comes by. After a while, they may get four or five visitors and then no-one again.

A lot of individuals think that all you have to do is put up a web site and it will be indexed by the search engines and then the world will find it. This is simply not true, although you may become indexed after a time. The problem with this tactic is that when people search on a term and the results come up, there are usually several hundred thousand listings. As an unknown site, yours will be close to the bottom of the pile and most people only look at the first page or two of results.

So, the trick is to get your web site listed on the front page of Google's search returns. Article marketing will help your web site rise in the rankings and become visible to your potential customers. It is far better to advertise your website so that it will be seen, than to have a flashy website that no-one will ever know about. You can add the bells and whistles later, if you still think it is worth it.

The explanation why writing articles works so well at increasing your website's visibility, is because of the way that Google works. Google attempts to rank websites on their reputation, which is supposed to give an idea of its worth. It measures popularity by the number of websites that link back to it. These are called backlinks.

If Google uncovers a backlink to your website, it checks your website for a reciprocal backlink to the website that holds one to you. Reciprocal backlinks are not as valuable as non-reciprocal backlinks. When you write an article, you are permitted to put two links back to your website (put one to your home page and one to another page).

If you submit that article to an article distribution site (and there are hundreds), other web masters could publish your article with its backlinks. The better the article, the more times it will be published, the more solo backlinks you will get and the higher you will climb in Google. The majority of money made on any search term will be made by the websites at the top of the first page.

There are some other ways of obtaining backlinks, but article marketing is by far the best, steadiest long term tactic for marketing a web site.

Who is likely to publish your article? Well, the distribution website for a start, but also newsletter writers, website owners, bloggers and others who need fresh content for their own businesses, but who might not have the time or know-how to write their own articles.

Post your article to article directories and websites like My Space, where they can be picked up, read and followed back to your website. See the article as a funnel to your website.

Sign up to blogs or create your own and post them there, but only post pertinent articles on other people's blogs.

When you have a quantity of interrelated articles, collate them into a book and give it away or sell it with your backlinks in place

Put a link on your website to an autoresponder which will send out your articles to people who sign up for it.

2. Increase Your Sales Today

There are fairly simple principles to follow if you would like to boost sales. In fact, it is so simple that it is hardly worth mentioning. The way to boost sales is to bring more visitors to see your product or an advert of your product.

If you can say that 5% of the population want to purchase your product, then to increase sales from 50 to 500, you simply have to get ten times as many people to notice you. Easy is it not?

The way the big professional firms accomplish that boost in viewers is to throw millions or even billions of dollars into an promoting budget and make use of nationwide or even worldwide promoting campaigns.

Assuming that you are not an owner of a firm that can afford to do this, the question is: how can you attract more visitors to your web site?

I am assuming here that you already have a website that converts traffic (in other words visitors) to sales at a certain rate, say 5%. So, how do you increase the number of visitors from 100 per day to 1,000 per day?

There are various ways of achieving this objective, but the exact technique varies depending on what you are selling. If you are selling a subscription or a high-cost service then you can afford to spend a bit more up front.

For instance, you could put an advert in the newsagent's window or in classified ads giving your telephone number and convert the curious into clientele when they phone you.

You will learn how much you need to spend to acquire a certain number of interested prospective clients and how many of these actually convert into customers. This is precious knowledge because it permits you to judge whether this type of marketing is correct for you and what your 'bang per buck' is.

However, this hypothesis goes for all forms of

promoting and if you are like most Internet sellers, you are working on a shoe string budget. Despite that, stick to first principles and keep as many statistics as you can think of. You might not know how to use those numbers yet, but something will occur to you.

As an instance, I record the details of the number of visitors to my web site each day and the number of clicks. That gives me an average: if a thousand people come to look, I make 80 sales. I also track the value of the sales and divide it by the clicks.

Then I know that, say, $240 worth of sales from 1,000 visitors equals an average of $3 a sale. Then I track the days of the week and by doing that I know that Saturday is more lucrative than Wednesday.

The days can vary by as much as 25%, so if you have an advertising budget of say $100 a week, it is better to go all-in on Saturday than $15 a day over the whole week because the costs are the same but the revenue is not. In short, if you want to create money on line. study the market as you would off line and put your promoting dollars where they matter the most.

3. Internet Marketing Secrets

You are reading this, so it is obvious that you already do some stuff on line, but how much do you use the Internet? Do you use it to its full potential? Do you just spend money on the Net or do you create money on the Internet too?

You might say that you have never spent a penny on line, but that would not be true, would it? You have a computer that you almost certainly use mostly for going on line and you pay for a broadband connection.

If you find yourself only surfing to use up free time, why not set yourself the goal of using the Net to pay for your monthly connection fees and your next (replacement) computer or a new laptop? That could be a project, a quest, a challenge, if you like.

If you have a surfeit of time on your hands this

would be a decent excuse to extend your knowledge of computers, the Net and business or business on line as well.

If you already have a business, on or off line, you ought to be using the Internet to advertise it. If you are unfamiliar with the on line ways of marketing, we can stick with traditional off line ways that have been imitated on line.

For example, there are thousands of free on line classified ad web sites. Just enter 'free classified ads' into Google and stand back!

However, classifieds are generally perceived as not being as effectual as their off line counterparts. This is because people spam these free ads web sites from all over the world merely for a free back link and so loads of the ads are irrelevant or not local.

Another kind of on line advertising copied from the 'real world' is banner marketing. Business people can pay to have a banner placed on a relevant website in order to promote their companies. It is equivalent to having a big advertisement in a newspaper.

Unfortunately, this kind of marketing does not work

on line so well as it does off line either. Specialists say that surfers expect things for free on line, so their eyes 'look through' banner adverts.

So how can you promote your business on line? Well, believe it or not, it by using the really top, up-market off line promoting techniques of having recommendations, reviews and pieces written about the goods that you are marketing. This would cost thousands or more in a newspaper, but it is practically free on line.

The number one best way of advertising on line is to write pieces on or about the subject of your products or company and posting them to article directories with your URL in the byline. This will give you a back link which Google values very highly in working out your firm's ranking in their search engine.

4. How to Monetize Your Traffic

Establishing your own e-commerce site is not the same as what it used to be. There are millions of competitors who are all too willing to get a larger share of the action, which means that anything you can come up with to increase your split will help, even if only a little..

We have got to admit to ourselves. The majority of us are in it for the money. We do not want to squander our time and endeavour just for the fun of it. Most site owners would not wait long to see their profits. While there are those who do not mind waiting, most would like their money right now..

It is common knowledge that without visitors we have no business. Like any business, without any clientele you don't get any orders. Traffic represents all the people that come to see to see what you have to for sale. The more surfers who see your products the more people there will be to buy them.

Nobody puts up an e-commerce site who doesn't want to make a profit. We have startup monies that need to be recouped. With consistent traffic, we at least have a fighting chance to accomplish that probability. Monetizing your traffic can make the most of your likelihood of making the best out of it.

Making Revenue out of your Traffic

The best and most proven system of earning a return out of your visitors is using advertising. The Internet provides hundreds of thousands upon hundred of thousands of surfers everyday. Most of them are searching for something. While some are merely looking for information, there is also a good proportion that is searching for something that they require.

The Internet has proven to be a very dependable source for finding whatsoever goods people desire. The Internet has made the world a smaller place; you can market a product from Istanbul and still find a buyer in the heart of Amsterdam.

Nevertheless, building traffic is not an easy task. You need to contend with a vast quantity of sites to create a good traffic flow. But if done successfully, this could generate plenty of possibilities. One of the benefits is monetizing your traffic flow.

So, to get to the nub of it, the more visitors you attract, the more likely you are to be considered as a desirable promoter. Basically, traffic equals sales. Advertising is the name of the game; with a good advertising plan you can use your traffic flow to your advantage.

When you have good traffic you have a good amount of prospective consumers, customers that are willing to pour money into your bank account.

This plan is called "pay-per-action". With every click a visitor of your site makes on an promotion link you will be remunerated, depending on your agreement with the merchant. It could be per click or per sale. Either way, the more traffic you create and the more clicks that happen, the more revenue you'll make.

What happens is, traffic generated from your site will be transferred to another site that can offer a product that you do not hold. There are lots of programs that can keep record and make records of transactions that was made feasible because of site linkage.

When purchases are made by customers that were provided by your site to their site, you receive a proportion of that sale. Affiliate programs would give you the benefit of monetizing your traffic without the actual need of carrying a solitary product.

There are so many ways and methods to monetize your traffic. All it takes is a lot of hard work and the desire to inaugurate a profit-earning site. The Internet is a veritable source of information, many tips and guides are offered everywhere on how to monetize your visitors and make your site a good money earner.

5. Ways to Build an Opt-in List

You have finally realized that you need a good opt-in list. After reading innumerable articles and sought expert advice and have read many success stories of people creating a small fortune with opt-in lists, you have at long last decided to have one of your own.

Then this happens, you believe you know everything there is to know about opt-in lists and have followed their advice to the letter but you still aren't able to make any money.

In fact, you may even be losing money. You may be hiring writers or there may be other costs incurred. Even if you have a large list, but only a fairly tiny percentage actually buys from you, you could still be losing money. You'll realize that after a few weeks, when you see your statistics and sales figures.

So what could have gone wrong? Why have others

succeeded where you have failed? The most common mistake is to jump straight right in. You chose a topic which you thought might be pretty popular and would earn you money. However, this is just not the case. Just because you write to people on the list, it doesn't mean they will buy.

Here I will offer more advice, for those who have started an opt-in list and have failed. You can rejuvenate your disastrous project. For those who are just starting off, here are three quick and easy ways to build a profitable opt-in list.

1] Get your customers to trust you and your products first. Just launching an opt-in list does not make you an expert or a believable supplier. Write many articles before you start an opt-in list. Write about any topic you know and have started and used for your site. Use forums to gain knowledge about your customers and their wants and needs and aim for those wants and needs.

Join forums from other sites as well. Provide expert tips and recommendations. When you feel that people trust you, you will be able to start your own opt-in list. You can build a customer base with other forum users. You can invite them to join your list.

Friends are always good customers. Put up a link to your site so that they can see what your business is all about.

The truth is, the money will only come in when consumers and subscribers believe in and trust you. They want a product or service that is good value for their money. People are not going to buy something because of your suggestion if they don't know you.

2] Find a product or service that people want and need. Although it may not be your strong suit, if you provide a service and product that you have researched and learned about well, you can put that over.

While it is true that it is best to sell something that you have an interest in, there are not many people who have the same interests exactly. Do your investigation well and you will see the profits come in. Also provide your subscribers with promotional material that they can actually use and pass around.

3] Make friends with other opt-in list users. This is beneficial especially if it is someone who has already started a thriving opt-in list. These are people that have experience in this venture and experience is still the best teacher. While there are many articles available on the Internet, there is nothing like getting a first hand account from someone you have faith in.

Experienced opt-in list users will be able to tell you what to do and what not to do because they have gone through it. While different problems crop up for different people, the general ideas can still be very helpful. There are many pitfalls to evade and these people will be able to tell you which ones.

Creating a profitable opt-in list doesn't happen overnight. There is much groundwork to do. Opt-in lists must be built from scratch, as your list grows, you should also uphold the quality of your list. Keep it organized and manageable. Get or hire help if need be, just make sure that your subscribers are happy and satisfied and they will be willing to buy from you one day.

6. Internet Business Opportunities

There are obvious benefits of having an Internet business over having a traditional business in a store on the high street. However, a traditional high street shop also has advantages. For instance, you have to be there every day or the store is not open and people will walk past your shop. The disadvantages are that you will have to stock the shop and pay rent.

An Internet business is cheaper to set up; you might not need stock and it can run and make money for a couple of days without you or anyone else being there. If you establish your Internet business properly. As with all well-organized jobs, a lot of the work goes on behind the scenes. Internet business opportunities are not different.

The benefits of Internet business opportunities over high street businesses are that potential earnings are limited only by the quantity of people online, not the number of people who walk down your street; start up costs are very low, although time spent setting up the business can be higher and you do not have to be present to make a sale, so you can sell twenty-four hours a day, seven days a week.

Internet sales are booming. In fact, the Baby Boomers were disinclined to give their credit card details over the Internet until banks promised immunity from Internet fraud. The children of the Baby Boomers have no such disinclination and neither do their children. Not only that, but as more and more previously 'poor' countries become industrialized, they too are using the Internet to shop on line.

When the Chinese and the Indians start shopping on line there will be a worldwide boost to sales the dimension of which has never been seen in world history. Both India and China have more than a billion inhabitants, many or whom are poor, but their economies are growing by about ten percent a year. How many of those people are going on the Internet every day with a credit card in their pocket?

They also want the items that Westerners have or want. They have seen them on TV and in the films.

They want new technology and very soon they will be purchasing it.

Hobbies are a good place to begin. Only individuals who have free time can indulge in hobbies. Poor people, I mean Third World poor people, only work and sleep. When Asia becomes rich enough to have time for hobbies, make sure that you are ready and now is the time to get ready.

Tourism is another good starting point. Many Asians are already going abroad. Usually in Asia and mostly in guided package tours, but the trend is there. Travel agencies, hotels, tour buses and related industries should get prepared.

If you are searching for Internet business opportunities the time has never been better. Within the next few years confidence will return in the West and credit cards will start coming out in the East. Now is the time to consider a career on the Internet and search out a couple of Internet business opportunities.

7. Affiliate Marketing Websites

In the first part of this article, we discussed creating affiliate marketing websites and how you ought to choose your products and plan your affiliate marketing website pages. The next stage is how to attract visitors (i.e. customers) to your affiliate marketing websites.

Selling on the Internet is what they call a 'numbers game', which means that only a small percentage of visitors to your affiliate marketing websites will become clients, so the first objective is to get a lot of surfers. The second goal is to raise the conversion rate of visitors to shoppers.

The secret to attracting visitors to your affiliate marketing websites is to have high quality content; therefore, this is the next job you must pay attention to in creating your affiliate marketing websites. There may be a number of other means that play a role in the success of your affiliate marketing websites, but good quality contents is at the top of the list. This will be just the explanation why surfers pick to enter your website. They want to get information and if they don't find it on your website, they will go somewhere else.

As a result, you have to write attention-grabbing articles related to your website as this will encourage them to come to your website more frequently. If you have already looked for affiliate programs that match your site, add links to the business sites and other excellent edifying websites.

Links contribute to how well you will be listed in the major search engines as well. In addition, build pages for the goods you are promoting, but don't just promote the products by putting hyped-up ads.

Keep your readers interested by frequently inserting plenty of pertinent and helpful information. This will encourage them to click the links in your affiliate business sites and buy the goods. Remember that no high-quality content means no frequent visitors, which means no sales and at the end of the day, no commission.

Keep your site simple although it must exhibit a touch of elegance in order to make it look more like a commercial website rather than a personal website. This should make it pleasing to the eye and consequently much more attractive to browse. To help you with the design, you could check out some of the successful online stores to get a better idea of how you can make your site look better.

One suggestion is to make sure you don't place too many banner adverts on your affiliate marketing websites, since these might sidetrack your site users and so, instead of clicking your advertisement, they may simply leave your site and look for another, more interesting website.

However, restricting the number of banners is not a problem, since banner adverts are not the only means of promoting your goods. Now your website is finished, submit its URL to the major search engines and lists to boost your number of visitors.

After all this, you must carry on learning. Learn about the use of keywords for search engine optimization and utilize them in your affiliate marketing websites' contents. Refresh your affiliate marketing websites frequently and insert original webpages. Make sure to inform your prospects about the latest updates to your affiliate marketing websites.

You can employ newsletters to accomplish this. The Internet is a huge resource of information about just about everything, make use of it. Carry on teaching yourself how to improve your affiliate marketing websites and soon you'll find yourself successful in affiliate marketing with websites.

8. Internet Marketing Tools

Many surfers are taking up Internet marketing for several reasons: maybe they think that their current career is at danger; maybe they do not like their current career; maybe they think that Internet marketing is easier than what they are doing now or maybe they only want to earn a bit of extra money on the weekend. Whatever the reason, they will have to learn how to make use of Internet marketing tools.

These Internet marketing tools may not all be quite obvious as Internet marketing tools to the newcomer to Internet marketing, so in the rest of this piece we will take a closer look at some of the less obvious, but better Internet marketing tools around.

The best Internet marketing tools, or at least most of them are: SEO, article marketing, content management, RSS, affiliate marketing, lists, Web2 and auto responders. There are others that used to help before, but which have waned in significance such as: Free For All lists, Safe Lists and Traffic Exchanges.

The point here is that some things that were touted as the bee's knees of Internet advertising a couple of years ago are not so effective now and new ways are being invented all the time, some of which are very useful like: Web2 and RSS. You need to keep your ear to the ground with regard to Internet marketing tools or you will miss current developments and fall behind.

SEO or search engine optimization is one of the best Internet marketing tools about because the principles, once studied, can be applied to any site for long-term improvement in the ranking stakes. Start with your domain name. Choosing the correct domain name is by far the most crucial step you can take in SEO. Make it pertinent to what you are trying to achieve.

For example, if you want to sell petrol powered model helicopters, try to get hold of a domain name with those words in the name like petrolpoweredmodelhelicopters.com. If you can not get that try to get petrolpoweredmodelhelicoptersforsale.com. Do not settle for petrolpoweredmodels.com even if you think that you might expand into other related models. Link the web sites instead.

Pick your keywords carefully and use them in your compositions. Needless to say, the domain name should become your foremost keyword or keyword phrase. Do not be tempted to use it ad nauseam, use it only where it fits in but make an effort to make it fit in. Reword sentences and paragraphs to accomplish this. In this article my keyword phrase or LTKW (long tail keyword) is 'Internet marketing tools' - see, I just got it in again :-)

Write web pages for your site including keywords and LTKW, but keep those pages unique to your web site. Then compose articles around and about the subject of your site, but do not mention your keywords in them or you will lose traffic on your keywords to other, larger businesses.

Post these articles, with links back to your site, on article directories. Hopefully, web masters of blogs and newsletters will choose these pieces and use them and you will gain backlinks, kudos and page ranking for your site.

The last of these Internet marketing tools is the list. Lots of people quote 'The money is in the list', but some marketers do not bother with a list. Most do but not all. If you want to build a list, add a box to your site so that visitors can sign up for your monthly newsletter and extraordinary offers.

9. Internet Scams and Making Money

If you have been on the Internet long enough to set up some kind of email address, you will probably have been invited to earn some extra money by filling in on line surveys.. These so-called paid on line surveys are aimed at the growing number of people who stay at home all day with a computer, little capital and no work. They are particularly aimed at stay at home mums and the unemployed.

It is possible to earn a few dollars a month from some of these on line survey businesses, but many of them are cons. They can make their money in a variety of ways, but usually the cash out figure for the person surveyed is quite high, often $50 or $100 It is hard to attain that figure at the rate of one $1 survey per week. However, they have you traipsing back and forth to their website in the hope that you will click on one of their adverts and they will get paid.

The first sign of a scam survey firm is the up front registration fee. This is typically less than $50 and seems a good deal if you are going to be earning the thousands of dollars that they 'promise'. Well, not really promise, because the disclaimer always states that you may not earn as much as the 'people' who have sent in the testimonials that you read plastered all over their web sites.

Testimonials from people like 'Mary T., New York', completely undetectable, unverifiable, probably fabricated 'people', who claim to be earning enough money completing on line surveys to pay off the mortgage, buy a big car and go on holiday in the Seychelles every year. Rule number one for avoiding on line scams: never pay a fee on the assurance of possibly earning money.

The cell phone rip-off is always very popular amongst con men and women. In this scam, you will be asked to authenticate that you are a real person by replying to a straightforward text message. What you are not told though is that you are texting a premium number which will probably cost you up to $5. The company is sure that you will not notice this charge, especially if you are pay-as-you-go and do not receive monthly bills.

Another popular dodge is where you are promised special offers or even cash for clicking on the banners of the site's 'partners'. You will be asked to seek more details by clicking on a banner. You may be promised 30% off or five cents for clicking. What you are not told is that you will be plagued from now to kingdom come by telesales people. Health insurance, pet insurance, free holidays, you name it. The only thing that you can be certain of is that you will end up paying more.

Then there is the free magazine con. You are offered a free magazine on an interesting topic of your choice. Again they ask for your telephone number. What they do not say is that your free magazine comes with a subscription to their magazine which costs $19.95. The payment will be made to your phone bill and you will probably never even notice it, which is what they are hoping for.

Never give out sensitive information over the Internet if you do not know who is receiving it. Phishing is also a profitable swindle, where an email purports to come from a bank or even Google or Yahoo. You are told that your account has been hacked and that you should confirm your details. As soon as you do, your account will be hacked sure enough.

10. The Different Types Of Affiliate Marketing

Marketing products with your affiliate code implanted in the hyperlink has been about for a decade or more, but it is even more common now than ever before. The principle, in a nut shell for those who do not already know, is that the distributor of the item supplies the marketer with a link to a product and within that link is a unique reference code which indicates the marketer. If your link is clicked and a transaction is completed, then the marketer gets paid.

With all the millions of new surfers coming on line every week, there is guaranteed to be some that is hoping to make some income on the side. And why not?

So, how can you go about making money from affiliate marketing? Well, there are a number of different types of affiliate marketing and it would be best if you acquaint yourself with them first.

When you have heard of the different kinds of affiliate marketing below, you will be in a better position to work out which one suits you and your website or style.

Pay Per Click (PPC) is popular with merchants and affiliates alike. This requires a lot of trust on behalf of both parties. The distributor has to believe that the clicks are genuine and the marketer has to believe that he will get remunerated for every click. Google's Adsense is a great illustration of PPC.

Pay Per Performance (PPF) is more popular with distributors than affiliates, because they do not get rewarded unless a specific action is taken by the visitor. There are essentially two different varieties of PPF:

Pay Per Sale (PPS), i.e. you do not get paid unless the merchant sells something and
Pay Per Lead (PPL) where you do not get paid unless your visitor hands over his email address

These are the most common types of advertising

preferred by those paying, because they only pay for what they get, but they are least well-liked by marketers because you can finish up doing a great deal of work for no money.

Then there are variations built into these basic types of affiliate marketing.

Multi-Tier Affiliate Marketing is where you, the marketer, the first affiliate in your line or marketing team can make sales, as above, but if you recruit others to do the same, they will be placed in your 'down-line' and you will get a percentage of every sale that they make too.

This can go many levels deep, but the percentage you earn will reduce also. It is a huge inducement to the novice, but these plans are typically very difficult to make work.

Recurring Payment Schemes normally involve subscriptions, but they can also correlate to sales completed by your former customers months or years later. This is no more than fair as you found the client in the first place. In fact, the system depends on cookies.

When your client makes the first purchase a cookie with your ID will be placed on his computer. If he returns, the distributor will look for the cookie to see if the sale should ascribed to anyone. So far so good, but what if the person has cleaned his cookies, like I do every day?

11. Sourcing Ebay Products

You could have already discovered that dealing on eBay can be fun and lucrative. But after you've cleared out your garage and attic, and auctioned off everything your spouse owns, where can you go to get new merchandise ideas?

Using EBay's Resources

Most people don't appreciate that eBay itself is in fact a terrific place to find product originating ideas. Besides being an easy selling venue with built-in traffic, it also contains a goldmine of useful data about what that traffic wishes to purchase.

One of eBay's best-kept secrets is their Seller Central page at www EBay.com/SellerCentral. Very few people, even Power Sellers, are conscious of this precious resource. Consequently, very few people are taking advantage of the tools accessible there:

• The merchandising calendar - this is a quality place to obtain sourcing leads because it shows you explicitly which products eBay will be marketing over the next few months. It gives you dates and tells you which item categories you need to list your product in for it to be displayed on eBay's homepage. When a user searches on that item, your auction item will pop right up.

• The hot items section - this is basically a monthly trend-watching report. It tells you what items are moving, producing more bids, and getting higher final prices. It lets you acquire a feel for where the demand is.

Whether you're looking for goods at a trade show or a rummage sale, Janelle Elms of eBay University, says, "Print this report and keep it with you at all times." She explains, "If you don't know what to sell, this will help focus and keep your mind targeted on what's moving on eBay."

• The hot categories sector - this resource takes the top categories and gives you advice on how to sell in those categories, insider secrets about your buyers, and trending information. For each category, there's a section called 'In Demand' that informs you not only the top-selling items in that category, but also the top keywords that buyers are using to find these items. Use those keywords in your listing titles. If you have any left over, put them in your description. Basically, eBay tells you what to sell and then informs you how best to list it.

Catering to Your Customers

Advises Elms, "Don't ever try to sell to the buyer what you think they need to own." Users are already telling you what they would like to buy - you simply have to listen. These tools show you what consumers are saying they would like and how they're saying they want to come across it. EBay users are ready to spend money with you - all you need to do is offer them what they're looking for.

12. Tips for Online Success

Businesses connected to the Internet have not stopped evolving. In the early days of the Internet (and it has only been around for about fifteen years), there was much more specialism in the field of web site design. In essence, there were graphic designers; web site promoters or marketers and the database specialists. Nowadays, these areas of expertise have blurred and most people who work on the Internet will take on all three jobs.

This is partially because the tools that are available to the DIY builders of web sites are so much better and because SEO (search engine optimization) techniques are more generally understood. Some of the most impressive web site creation software will not only counsel you on SEO techniques as you are building your web site, but it will also let you program in several languages, without you even having to be conscious of the fact that you are writing in PHP or ASP instead of HTML (which is the language that most web sites are written in).

This simplicity of web site creation and SEO permits owners of micro businesses to focus more on sales than teaching themselves programming languages and it also allows professional web site creators to develop high-quality web sites more quickly therefore more economically.

I think that it is better to spend, say $250, on good web site construction software than it is to pay someone $250 for a good web site. Web sites need maintenance and they have to be modified and up-dated to keep them looking novel and vibrant. You cannot keep going back to the programmers every week for tiny $5 up-dates. They will not be amused unless they work for you in-house, in which case you would probably not be reading this article.

You need to be able to carry out these changes yourself and you will want to make them quickly, so you might as well get good HTML editing software in the first instance. If you do that, then you may as well build your own web site too.

When you are designing your first website, try not to

over complicate things. The best HTML editors have a selection of templates for you to choose from. Pick one of these and just change the colours, if you decide to. The HTML editor that I use has about a hundred built in templates and they are all fully customizable by several clicks of the mouse.

Your web site should be pleasant on the eye, of course, but it should not take more than a number of seconds to load. You may have 32 MBps, but most of the world is still down around the 256 kbps mark. Keep that in mind when you are adding fancy graphics, music or video links. People will not wait more than a few seconds for your site to load, especially if it commences playing your favourite music at them too.

So, when you are designing your web site, remember the objective of the web site. Be clear on that and stay focused. You do not need bells, whistles, music, video and Flash graphics, if you are trying to sell cheap nylons, but you could have to have them if you are trying to sell your expertise as a web site designer.

Do not have any diversions from your chief objective. For instance, on my first web site, I thought it would be nice to keep people amused while they were thinking of buying, so I had Sudoku, hangman, crosswords and the like there. People played the games and then clicked through to the Sudoku website to play more games. Sales plummeted. Keep your hard-earned visitors on your web site by not giving them any links to click away on except Google Adsense, for which you will get paid anyway.

13. What Is Viral Marketing?

The idea of viral marketing is one of the more recent methods of marketing to come to the Internet. As the word 'viral' suggests, it depends on people passing your advertising material around like a cold. It would normally go from friends and colleagues to their friends and colleagues ad infinitum.

You can believe that if I sent a message to all the people in my address book and they did the same, the message would probably reach a million people in a month. All free of charge.

Viral marketing is low cost and can be fast and far reaching, if you use the proper marketing medium, but it does tend to be unfocused. That is to say, you do not know who is going to receive your viral ad, so you do not know if that person will be interested or not.

You can draw various conclusions, if you choose your material properly though. Say, you had a web site on craft work. You could send out a free knitting pattern to all your acquaintances and to those other people who have given you permission to do so (no spamming, please). Append the URL of your website at the bottom and tell the recipients that they may forward it on to anyone they know who would like it.

Bingo! Now you know that most of the recipients after the first wave that you sent out yourself will be interested in crafts and / or knitting. It is also pretty safe to presume that most of them will be older women with computers. If you marked your return URL with a code by sending them to a web page like viral-ad1-knitting.html and had a sign-up box their for a newsletter, you would soon have a list of older, computer literate women who like knitting or and other crafts. That information would be of use.

Different companies send out different things. It might be a free report on smoking or catching trout or bicycle maintenance. Some people simply send out jokes. Sending out jokes or pictures is not targeted but you can see how other things are very focused.

Hotmail developed this strategy and they maintain that they went from zero subscribers to twelve million in eighteen months. That is some record to beat. Look at the bottom of a lot of the email circulars that you get and you will in all probability still see Hotmail's viral marketing.

This is the best viral marketing system, but you must append you URL to something of value, you friends will not want to send junk or sales blurb to their friends and family. Keep the emails informative, useful or amusing, is the best strategy.

Very similar to this technique is the use of a sigfile (short for 'signature file'). Write a snappy little one or two line file with your URL at the end. Outlook, Outlook Express and most of the others will append this sigfile to the bottom of your emails automatically.

This is a good method of getting your URL out to thousands of people a month, especially if, when you write to say, your Mum, she forwards it to all your brothers and sisters, aunties and uncles.

It is a simple, yet free viral marketing tool that many

people overlook. By the way, use the same sigfile in the posts you make on blogs. You do not make any? Shame on you, you should. Search Google for related blogs like - blogs knitting - and sign up to a few.

Then read the posts and submit comments with your sigfile. Hundreds will read them and some will click through, if you are not too boring. Do not bore people on blogs by promoting yourself.

14. The Secrets Of Internet Marketing

You are obviously already on the Internet for some things like reading articles and probably email. Maybe even investigation and discussion groups. Or Facebook or one of the other look-alikes, but have you thought about utilizing your time on the Internet to make some money?

Once you choose a business model, no matter which one you choose, the time will come when you want to tell the world about it in order to attract sales. In traditional business terminology, advertising, promoting or marketing, whatever you prefer to call it meant spending lots of money. National advertising was a huge enterprise involving television and the press. Global advertising would bankrupt many national firms.

However, that has all changed now and one person sitting at a rented computer in an Internet Cafe can contact the whole world's online population. This is quite a stunning thought. A poor Thai artist who used to have a difficult time selling paintings on the beach road can now sell in New York, London and Paris all at the same time. Internet marketing is genuinely remarkable and it is virtually free too.

So, where would you start your Internet marketing campaign? Remember that some forms of advertising are more suitable for physical products and others are better at lead generation, so bear that in mind when you plan your Internet marketing campaign.

There are free classified ads. Hundreds of companies will allow you to place one or two free ads a week on their website. Some will charge if you want to place more but others do not. Keep it free by putting free ads with a dozen publications. Look to see whether the publication is a newspaper (off line) or a newsletter (on line).

Many local newspapers accept one free ad per week per customer over the Internet. When you compose these ads, put a distinguishing word or code into each one, so that when you get a sale or reply you know where it came from. Keep recomposing your ads and stop putting them where they do not work. Keep records of what you are doing and where.

Write a signature file (sigfile) and append it to all of your postings and emails. The sigfile should be a one or two line advert and your website or email address at the end. Many people ignore this simple, set-and-forget, free marketing instrument.

Join groups, like Yahoo Groups, of people who would appreciate your products. There are thousands of groups and blogs you can join. Just Google your interest. Post polite questions and join in discussions. Do not advertise, but add your sigfile after each post. People will become aware of it and come to see what you are doing.

Write articles on and around your pet subject and leave an extended sigfile at the bottom with up to two links. Article marketing is a very effectual means of helping people understand a problem or amusing them, while your advert sits at the bottom the page waiting for the curious to click it. You can post copies of your article to any of thousands of blogs and article databases on the Internet. A Google search will reveal them.

15. Sales Marketing Strategy

Each product has to have a sales marketing strategy to support it. You can occasionally promote a few items together like a table and chairs, but any device for which you do not have a sales marketing strategy is doomed to failure.

Let me put it simply, if you went out one day and noticed that someone was selling his whole stock of bicycle tyres cheap because they were going bankrupt and you purchased them, who would know except you and the person you bought them from? And he is not going to want them back!

You may say: 'But I would not do that. I would put an advert in the paper'. Well, that is your advertising strategy. I am not saying that it is a decent one, but at least it is something. Something to build on really.

The first thing to think about is who your target

market is and how can you best reach them. The answers to these two questions will permit you to choose whether you are going to concentrate on or off line sales. Never forget that the vast bulk of sales are off line, although the on line market is growing every day.

If you have a shed load of bicycle tyres, for example, you would probably be better off advertising them in the classifieds section of the local paper. Or you could advertise a one-off garage sale of cheap bicycle tyres or you could take them to a car boot sale. In your spare time, you could create a small web site, but in this instance off line sales are more probable than on line sales.

If however, you hook up with a bicycle tyre company that is willing to drop-ship (i.e. deliver) from their warehouse for you then a car boot or garage sale is useless to you. In this instance, you should go straight on line, create an automated sales and payment processing page and promote it on line by the various methods on hand.

If you really want to, you could back up the on line sales with a bit of off line advertising. For instance, you could put a postcard in the newsagent's window promoting that your web site has a stock of cheap bicycle tyres that can be delivered to the customers' door. Then only add the URL of your web site.

Your sales advertising strategy must be tailored to what you are trying to sell. In other words, you have to have a great deal of promoting tactics so that you can select the ones that are correct for your product. No one sales advertising strategy is ever going to fit all the products. Therefore, if you rely on only one sales marketing strategy you will not succeed.

In summary, once you have your irresistible product finished for sale, sit down and think about who will purchase it and how you can reach them - i.e. how you can tell them that you have what they would like. Then draw up a plan - yes, I mean write something down! Write down how you are going to achieve this and set down while the stages of your sales promoting strategy have to be completed by.

It is only by having a solid sales promoting strategy that you can cite that you will succeed in advertising. Failing to plan is tantamount to planning to fail.

16. What Is Article Marketing?

Article marketing is the writing of articles that are pertinent to the subject of the web site that you wish to promote. It works because the writer is allowed to append two URL's to the articles, normally at the bottom, which will permit the reader to click through for more information.

Therefore, if you desired to promote a web site on cooking, you might write a series of articles on ways of cooking or using various kitchen gadgets.

If you send these articles to a general article database, you can assume a pretty low click through rate (CTR), but if you posted it to a cooking blog, you could look forward to a higher CTR.

The good thing is that everyone who clicks through will know what they are likely to see on your site, so they are focused visitors and focused visitors are more likely to turn into customers.

The articles that you submit to webmasters of blogs and article databases usually want to approve them for length and content, but if you are honest, that is hardly ever a problem Another advantage of article marketing is that these webmasters never shunt your article off their web site when new arrive.

They may place them into archives, but the archives are still readable and scannable by Google and this is an important point too.

You see, Google rates web sites on their popularity and one of the methods it uses to judge popularity is how many links there are on the Internet pointing back to it. They are called backlinks. People found this out and attempted to work around it (and still do) by exchanging backlinks.

However, Google rates one-way backlinks higher than reciprocal links. An article on a blog gives you two one-way backlinks until the blog goes under. If you pick where you post astutely, this might never happen.

Google also checks to see if the host of your link is

applicable to your site, so it is worth posting to sites that are pertinent to yours and Google awards extra merit if the site having your link is an authority site, that is, a top site on that topic.

If you post an article to an article database and a leading authority site or newsletter on that topic picks it up and prints it, you will get loads of bonus points from Google, shoot up in the ranking, get loads of visitors and more customers.

The message is to write informative, pertinent articles and post them where they can be found. By this I mean, use the largest article databases, because that is where the top people go to look for content if they are stuck and also post your article to blogs that are relevant to the topic of your article, which should be relevant to the theme of your website, which should be relevant to what you are trying to promote.

I recently had one of my articles picked up. I received 3,450 plus visitors to my web site within two hours and 256 of them became customers. If only it could be done every day. The thing is, it can, if you get the strategy right. Stay focused.

17. Starting Your Internet Business

Embarking on any new business venture is costly, stressful and arduous. Anyone who has started up a traditional business or an Internet business will know that there is a lot of work that goes on that the customer does not know about. There was a lot of graft done before the doors opened or the website launched for the first time. Launching your Internet business will take a lot out of you, in particular if you aspire to be up and running quickly.

Here are a few tips I can give you to get you going:

Make a start-up strategy. Write things down and tick them off when you have completed them. A start-up strategy for a new Internet business could look like this:

1] identify a need

2] work out how you can fulfil that need by finding a trustworthy existing supplier or having the merchandise made for you

3] produce a means of showing your prospective clients that you have what they need and produce a means for them to purchase it immediately (a website and a shopping cart).

4] ascertain your potential customers and tell them how they can solve their problem

5] work out some practical goals. Define where you want to be in three, six, nine, twelve and fifteen months ahead. Keep checking your results against these goals and endeavour to meet them. If you do not, work out why. If you do, reward yourself and upgrade your goals. Do not be over ambitious.

Select your domain (web site) name very cautiously. I only just met someone who had clearly put a great deal of effort into a blog and it looked great, but a quick check showed that the name of the blog/website had not been searched for on Google even once in the previous month. Do not permit that to happen to you.

If you had not considered the status of the name of your website before you created it, grab the bull by the horns and change it. Relaunch your web site with the new name. Swallow your pride. You can keep the content.

Build a good-looking web site. You can have the web site crafted for you, but you will still need to be able to revise it, so you either need a working knowledge of HTML or you have to have a good HTML editor. Personally, I do not desire to be a programmer, so I went for the best HTML editor that I could find. I use it each day and I love it.

You will need to host your web site. This is cheap enough, less than a hundred dollars a year, but you have to find a good host. Check how often they are down and check their other promises too. Check for statistics. Most supply statistics included in the price, but some take it out of the package to sell them individually at a high cost.

Once you have come this far, you will have to tell people that your web site is out there, because it is a myth that it will be discovered whatever. Millions and millions are spent on search engine optimization and traffic generation and there are hundreds of books you can purchase and study on the subject. It is a gigantic and ever-changing technique that requires a study and another article all unto itself

18. The Rôle of PLR in Internet Marketing

The Internet has been around for more than twenty-five years now, but there are still a lot of novice or would-be sales people who don't realise that Internet marketing is basically the same as any other type of marketing, except that you have more possibilities and that it can be cheaper.

Cheaper? Cheaper to reach more people who might be interested in whatever you have to sell – your potential customers - and on an industrial scale. Traditionally, a salesperson would be advertising to the inhabitants of his or her town. Television increased the scope to nationwide, but the Internet has made that global.

If you are a one-man band, this potential can be daunting, and you will soon come to understand that you are just not able to source your goods; create and maintain your website; write sales literature for it; take orders and dispatch them; deal with inquiries, complaints and returns; plus maintain records for tax purposes, stock, etc., etc., all on your own. You will soon decide that you need help.

There are two ways to go: taking on (more) staff, or outsourcing work.

Taking on staff will free you up to learn about corporation tax, sales taxes, payroll, income tax, workers' rights, health and safety, and other employment laws, whereas outsourcing will only mean a little more paperwork, It will actually create more time for you.

What you outsource is obviously up to you, but I am going to recommend that one of the things that you could outsource quickly and cheaply is the writing of your sales material and website content. By 'website' here, I am including the far more interactive and responsive blog. This is the easiest and cheapest way of getting your Internet-based business up and running quickly.

If you have gone down this route, like it or not, you are now an Internet Marketer with a mail order business. Congratulations!

There are five basic points that every Internet Marketer has to to learn about the mail order business in order to increase their profits:

1. that the Internet is just another (or perhaps the most superior) vehicle for direct response marketing, but it contains within itself the potential to make you rich! However, because the marketplace is so huge, and therefore has many participants in it, it evolves extremely quickly.
2. that there are hardly any markets where fashion or current trends do not play a rôle, and you will need to keep abreast of those fast-changing trends
3. that prices move quickly, some tend to rise, whereas those in older technology fall
4. international law changes – bans, embargoes, tariffs and trade wars are becoming more and more common
5. it has never been easier to reach so many people so quickly

When you have sorted these obstacles out, you may like to outsource your marketing as well as drop-shipping, but in the beginning, you will probably need to provide your own marketing material. This raises two questions: do you have the talent to write it, and, if so, do you have the time to write it?

If not, then again, you have two possible solutions: either hire someone to write bespoke articles for you, or find relevant off-the-peg articles and modify them to suit your needs.

The name given to these off-the-peg articles is PLR, which stands for Public Label Rights, and once again, there are two sorts: the first kind is usually free, but old articles that have been around for quite some time, and can be spotted on numerous sad-looking blogs; and the second, so-called fresh material, which has to be bought, although it is usually fairly cheap. Both kinds are often bundled into niche packages, and should be fine-tuned to perfectly suit your business.

The big difference is that the articles that have been used hundreds of times will need a lot of re-writing since so many variations already exist, whereas the the second can be turned around a lot more quickly.

Since these niche packages of PLR often cost less than $10 for a set of ten articles, it is hardly worth going for the free option, because your time is worth more than the cost of rewriting a free article as extensively as would be necessary to render it unique.

What sort of niche PLR packages are there? The range is unbelievable, there will not be much that a person can sell that will not be covered by a group of PLR articles somewhere. You will need to type something like: "[your product] PLR articles" (with the inverted commas) into a search engine. However, if you want to dive right in, even if it's only to have a look at some examples of niche PLR packages, you could do worse than try Megan Publishing Services (http://meganthemisconception.com).

Megan Publishing Services has fresh PLR for Internet Marketing purposes organised into 125+ niche packages of about fifteen articles of roughly 500-600 words a piece, which is the recommended size for an Internet article. It also has the same PLR packages in several languages, if you want to go down that road. Any smaller and the search engines might ignore it, and too much longer and the reader might give up before the end, modern attention spans being what they are.

Once you have your finely-tuned, modified article, you should place it on your website, and promote that page to your previous customer list, your website followers and the social media. After a few days, when the search engines know that the article originated from your website, you could copy it to whichever other locations you have deemed fit. These are probably specific to the industry you have chosen to market to: games, women's fashion, auto accessories, or whatever. You might also like to post the article to an Article Directory, which is a repository for pieces that the author is willing to share with other website owners. In effect, the other webmasters reprint your article on their site as a free guest article, but we'll leave that topic for another day.

19. Modern Internet Marketing Tools

Two modern Internet Marketing tools that will surely make your business life a lot easier are autoresponders and newsletters. I will come to what they are and how to use them later, but first you should know that these tools have actually been around for decades, so in that sense they are not that modern, but they are more sophisticated now. As an example, Windows 10 is a modern interface, despite the fact that Windows has been around for thirty years or more.

An autoresponder and a newsletter are essential communications tools, and communication is essential to Internet Marketing. After all, you will probably never meet more than just a few percent of your customers face to face, if that, so you will need to keep on top of emails.

And we all know what that means. Most people who use the Internet a lot can expect fifty to a hundred junk emails every day, and even a small business will probably receive ten times that. It is not only time consuming, but it is a largely time wasting, laborious and depressing job... but it has to be done, day after day, after day, after day. It is true that a decent email client can learn to distinguish which email you are likely to want to read and which ones you probably definitely do not.

Thunderbird is very good at learning your junk email preferences and obeying them. However, there is more that you can do.

Autoresponders

An autoresponder is like a mailing clerk. It is highly efficient at sorting your email into different pigeon holes. It can do this in several ways, but basically, it looks for a key word, words or phrase in the text, header or address lines, and files it accordingly.

That is enough to be grateful for all in itself, however, you do not need an autoresponder to just do that, Thunderbird can do that and it's free. An autoresponder will actually answer that mail with a preset reply that you have written previously and loaded into it. You may have come across the 'Out of office' reply. You have sent a message to someone, and you get an instant reply that they are not at work at that moment. This is a simple autoresponder at work.

One thing to say here is that that message will still arrive at that person's desk when he or she returns to work, but they are letting you know that the reply will be delayed.

Thunderbird can do that too. However, a proper autoresponder will do far more. For example, it can follow up on the original reply. Let's say someone asks for your catalogue. The autoresponder will send it. Then, if you want, say, three days later it can send another message asking whether it was received, and advising to check the junk email if not, or click 'this button' to have it resent. A week later, it might ask whether they require assistance with ordering. I think you get the idea, and every time that it receives a reply, it will give an appropriate response following a kind of flowchart that you have designed.

An autoresponder can even personalise emails with names, dates, addresses and the like, all gleaned from a database or even the incoming email and it will save that data for future use.

When you start using one, you will wonder how you ever managed before.

Newsletters

A company newsletter is a publication that goes out regularly to inform a group of interested people about new situations... usually new products or services. It would be sent to a list of people who have asked to receive such information. Sending the newsletter to people who have not requested it is called spamming, and we are all sick of it, aren't we?

This newsletter will save you having to write to everybody individually, and worrying whether you have left anybody out. It will also personalise each email with the person's name and other details as you desire.

A good question would be where you obtain the list of recipients from. Well, you put a note at the bottom of every email and every publication you send out, asking people whether they want to sign up. However, it is also legitimate to use the list of names that your autoresponder has collected once.

That is, you can transfer every name over to the newsletter list once, as long as there is an 'unsubscribe' button, so that they can opt out of the newsletter. This why you can transfer the names over only once. Otherwise, you risk being seen as pushy, or even a spammer... and we all know how bad that is, don't we?!

These two modern Internet Marketing tools will run like a well-oiled machine every minute of every day to keep your business in peak communications condition, leaving you with more time to get on with something else.

20. PLR Ebook Providers

PLR ebook providers are a source of useful, relevant, important information! Find out more about this undervalued resource below.

PLR stands for Private Label Rights. This means that someone else has created an article on a topic, which includes the research and the writing. If the article fits in with the requirements of what you would like to write about, then it is potentially useful to you. The authors of such articles give, or sell, you permission to use their content in your publication, and then sell copies of it under your own name as if you had written it.

What Are PLR Ebooks?

Many PLR Ebook providers sell bundles of targeted PLR articles in the form of ebooks. Such ebooks may contain ten to twelve PLR articles on closely related, niche subjects.

Why Should You Buy PLR Ebooks?

Two of the reasons why writers and publishers buy PLR ebooks are that they are a fast and cheap way of obtaining content for a publication. For example, if you see a great skin care product that you would like to promote, you can either spend days researching and writing a dozen articles on the subject, or you can spend $20 on pre-written material and start selling immediately.

The Pros & Cons Of PLR Ebook Providers

There are various pros and cons of using PLR ebook providers. However, they are basically the same as when buying any product. Quality is of prime importance. In the case of PLR, this means material that has been diligently researched, professionally written and not oversold. In other words, you don't want your article to be read on dozens of competitors' websites around the Internet. This is called fresh content.

Where To Go For More Information About PLR Ebooks

If you're looking for more information about PLR ebooks, then you should check out our collection of 125 niche PLR ebooks on this blog. Ours are unique for the reasons that they have been written by a professional novelist, and many of the ebooks exist in several languages, which means that you can sell to other countries with confidence.

Conclusion on PLR Ebook Providers

There are plenty of places online where you can buy niche PLR ebooks. However, most of them have been poorly written, overspun, and oversold. No other PLR ebook provider except Megan Publishing Services offers niche PLR ebooks written by a professional novelist and translated by professional native translators, so that sales campaigns can be run simultaneously in several countries.

21. About the Author

Owen Jones, Amazon Best-Selling Author from Barry, Wales, has lived in several countries and travelled in many more. While studying Russian in the USSR in the '70's, he hobnobbed with spies on a regular basis; in Suriname, he got caught up in the 1982 coup; and while a company director, he joined the crew of four as the galley slave to sail from Barry to Gibraltar a home-made concrete yacht, which was almost rammed by a Russian oil tanker and an American aircraft carrier.

"I am a Celt, and we are romantic", he said when asked about his writing style, "and I firmly believe in reincarnation, Karma and Fate, so, sayings like 'Do unto another...', and 'What goes round comes around' are central to my life and reflected in my work. I write about what I see, or think I see, or dream... and, in the end it is all the same really". He speaks seven languages and is learning Thai, since he lives in Thailand with his Thai wife of fifteen years.

His first novel, *Daddy's Hobby* is from the seven-part series 'Behind The Smile: The Story of Lek, a Bar Girl in Pattaya', but his largest collection is 'The Megan Series', twenty-three novelettes on the psychic development of a teenage girl, the subtitle of which, 'A Spirit Guide, A Ghost Tiger and One Scary Mother!' sums them up nicely. He has written fifty novels and novelettes, including: *Dead Centre*; *Andropov's Cuckoo*; *Fate Twister*; *The Disallowed* (a philosophical comedy); *Tiger Lily of Bangkok*; and *A Night in Annwn* (Annwn being the ancient Welsh word for Heaven). Many have been translated into foreign languages and narrated into audio books.

He sums his life up thus: "Born in the Land of Song, Living in the Land of Smiles".

Contact Details

Facebook: OwenJonesWriter –
Twitter: @owen_author
Blog: Megan Publishing Services

This book is part of the 'How to...' series of 125 manuals by Owen Jones.
The whole series can be found on Megan Publishing Services at:
http:/meganthemisconception.com

www.ingramcontent.com/pod-product-compliance
Ingram Content Group UK Ltd.
Pitfield, Milton Keynes, MK11 3LW, UK
UKHW021647190726
13853UKWH00001B/105

9 788835 461791